Ollie and Mollie
Meet New Friends

Written and Illustrated by

Betty Oliver

Betty Oliver 2022

Fulton Books, Inc.
Meadville, PA

Published by Fulton Books 2021

ISBN 978-1-63860-315-3 (paperback)
ISBN 978-1-63860-317-7 (hardcover)
ISBN 978-1-63860-316-0 (digital)

Printed in the United States of America

For my twin sister, Cathy Peyton

My art teacher, Mike Lane

And all the animal lovers in the world

Contents

Crocodile 1

Koala 2

Peacock 3

Owl 4

Pigs 5

Rooster 6

Chimp 7

Sloth 8

Tortoise 9

Red-Eye Tree Frog...10

Bear 11

Fox 12

Giraffes 13

Zebras 14

Horses 15

Elephants 16

Kangaroo 17

Wallaby 18

Lion 19

Cheetah 20

Eagles 21

Jellyfish 22

Shark 23

Rabbits 24

Dogs 25

Cats 27

Puffins 28

Penguins 29

About the Author 30

Ollie and Mollie are two penguins who have decided to go on a new adventure. They both want to meet other animals and see how they live. The penguins want to decide if the animals they meet are friendly or not. Ollie and Mollie want to learn about the sounds they make, the foods they eat, and what makes each animal so unique.

Ollie exclaimed, "I am scared, Mollie, of that crocodile."

Mollie replied, "You don't need to be because we are not going to be swimming in the water with him."

Ollie asked, "What kind of animal is a crocodile?"

Mollie answered, "It is the world's largest living reptile."

Ollie whispered, "I don't want him to see us because once he is close, swoosh! He might grab us for a meal."

Mollie asked, "What animals are in the trees?"

Ollie replied, "Mollie, that is a koala bear and its baby koala called a joey. The baby crawls into his mother's pouch right after birth and stays there for six months."

Mollie declared, "Ollie, you and I were chicks once and lived with our parents for seven weeks. Some penguins live with their parents up to thirteen months."

"Peep, peep!" shouted Ollie.

"How I would love to be a chick again."

Ollie shouted, "Wow, look at that fancy peacock with its colorful tail!

Mollie declared, "The peacock is trying to get the attention of a peahen, a female peacock."

Ollie remarked, "He certainly has my attention!"

Mollie stated, "Eventually, the peacock's long tail feathers fall out, but they will grow back the next year."

Ollie asked, "Can a peacock fly?"

Mollie answered, "The bird flies just fine but not very far."

Ollie concluded, "I hope we meet more elegant peacocks along the way."

Mollie noticed, "It is getting darker outside. Look, I see a stunning owl!"

Ollie replied, "I think the owl saw us coming because like all owls, he can turn his head around to look directly behind him in both directions."

Mollie whispered, "Listen, can you hear the owl hooting?"

Ollie answered, "Yes, it sounds so mysterious."

Mollie asked, "I wonder what an owl eats."

Ollie replied, "He eats mice, rabbits, and sometimes raccoons."

Mollie declared, "I like the beautiful owl, but I think it is time to meet another creature."

"Oink, oink," whispered the pigs.

"What squeaky sounds those pigs make!" exclaimed Mollie.

"I would like to have the pink pig as my pet," stated Ollie.

"Pigs are smarter than dogs and are very clean animals," responded Mollie. "They would make excellent pets."

"They like belly rubs," declared Ollie.

"Maybe we can all get our tummies rubbed while we are here," suggested Mollie.

"Ollie, I heard sounds from that rooster and hen," stated Mollie.

"Cock-a-doodle-doo!" shouted the rooster.

"Cluck," murmured the hen.

"What is the difference between a rooster and a hen?" asked Ollie.

"If it crows, it's a rooster," answered Mollie. "If it lays an egg, it's a hen."

"I like roosters and hens because they have wonderful memories and can recognize people they know," declared Ollie.

"Squawk, squawk," answered Mollie.

"You better not squawk too loudly if you want the roosters and hens to like you," whispered Ollie.

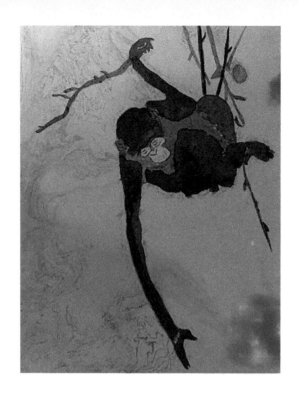

Ollie exclaimed, "Look at that cool chimp in the tree!"

Mollie declared, "I love watching him swing from the branches."

Ollie replied, "They love the fruit in trees, but they also eat termites, small ant-like insects."

"I am glad we like fish to eat," said Mollie.

Ollie whispered, "It sounds like the chimp is whimpering."

Mollie noticed, "I think he is reaching out to us."

Ollie shouted, "Look, Mollie, at that adorable animal living in the treetops!"

Mollie replied, "It's a three-toed sloth."

Ollie asked, "I wonder how long he stays in the tree."

Mollie answered, "Would you believe seven days? The sloth comes down to go to the bathroom and then goes right back up the tree."

Ollie declared, "I heard they are very slow, and it can take a month to digest one meal."

Mollie blurted, "Wow! We are fortunate that we can eat whenever we want."

Mollie exclaimed, "Look at those huge tortoises! I wonder what they eat."

Ollie answered, "They eat plants such as cactus, grass, flowers, and fruits."

Mollie asked, "Did you know these huge tortoises nap about sixteen hours each day?"

Ollie cried out, "Wow, I did not know that! Oh, look at that little iguana behind the turtle."

Mollie declared, "Maybe we can hang out with him. He is more our petite size."

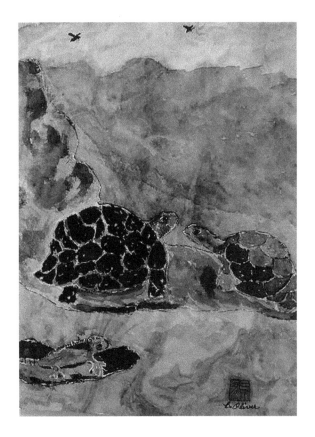

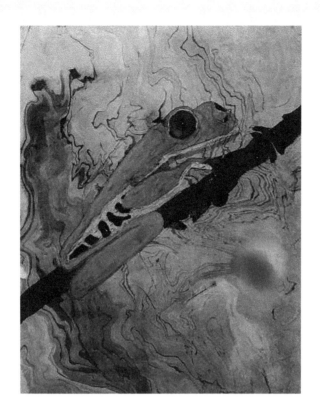

"I love meeting all these different animals," declared Mollie.

"Mollie, I wish I had vibrant red eyes like that tree frog. By the way, is he poisonous?" asked Ollie.

"Would you believe he is not poisonous? He can change color according to his mood," answered Mollie. "What an amazing animal he is!"

"Jingle, jingle!"

"I hear the red-eyed tree frog climbing in the trees," whispered Ollie.

"Maybe he will be our friend," wished Mollie.

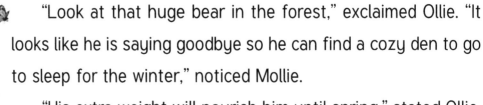

"Look at that huge bear in the forest," exclaimed Ollie. "It looks like he is saying goodbye so he can find a cozy den to go to sleep for the winter," noticed Mollie.

"His extra weight will nourish him until spring," stated Ollie.

"His thick fur will keep him warm in the winter," replied Mollie.

"I love meeting our new friend," declared Ollie.

"Bears are smart and have wonderful memories," offered Mollie.

"I bet he will never forget us!" shouted Ollie.

"Look at that large red fox," declared Mollie.

"I love his bushy tail!" exclaimed Ollie.

"The red fox sheds its fur every year," explained Mollie.

"That is called molting," stated Ollie.

"He can run swiftly through the woods," expressed Mollie. "The fox runs like a leaping wave."

"The red fox is ready to pounce on other animals," alleged Ollie. "He started pouncing when he was very young."

"Maybe we can pounce for fun," suggested Mollie.

"As long as we don't pounce on each other," whimpered Ollie.

Ollie declared, "Look at how gentle the giraffe and her calf are."

Mollie replied, "I love giraffes. Do you know how tall they are?"

Ollie answered, "Would you believe they are sixteen feet tall. The giraffes use their long necks to reach leaves on tall trees."

Mollie stated, "Giraffes can sleep standing up. They spend most of their time eating."

Ollie responded, "Let's stay and relax with the giraffes for a while."

"I love the zebras' brilliant black-and-white stripes," admired Mollie.

"Each zebra has different stripes, which helps them to recognize each other," replied Mollie.

"I like that the zebra is resting his head on the other one," mentioned Ollie.

"Since zebras sleep standing up, they like resting their heads on each other to feel safer," stated Mollie.

"It looks like the zebras are looking at us," declared Ollie.

"That's because they have excellent eyesight and can see everything around them," answered Mollie.

"I am so thrilled that we came to Africa to meet giraffes and zebras," expressed Ollie.

"I love meeting the stunning horses," declared Mollie.

"They appear healthy and strong," observed Ollie. "Horses are herbivores, only eating plants."

"Look at them gallop!" exclaimed Mollie. "Horses gallop at around twenty-seven miles per hour."

"Horses can run quickly after birth," stated Ollie.

"They can sleep both standing up and lying down," alleged Mollie.

"I wish we could learn to ride them," expressed Mollie.

"Of course we can with practice," answered Ollie.

"Listen, I hear the elephants roaring," whispered Ollie. "Elephants communicate and hear each other from up to five miles away."

"I wonder what elephants use their unique trunks for," asked Mollie.

"Elephants use their trunks for picking up objects, eating, drinking water, and breathing underwater," answered Ollie.

"Isn't it lovely how the baby elephant will hold on to his mother's trunk?" replied Mollie. "It reminds me of a child holding his mother's hand."

"We better go. The elephants are hungry since they eat sixteen hours a day," declared Ollie.

Ollie asked, "Is that a tiny kangaroo in her pouch?"

Mollie answered, "The precious baby kangaroo is called a joey, and he stays in his mother's pouch for around six months after he is born."

Ollie exclaimed, "Hop! I wish I could hop like a kangaroo!"

Mollie responded, "The kangaroo's tail acts like a third leg helping him move. He hops as fast as the speed of lightning."

Ollie questioned, "I wonder how far they can hop."

Mollie declared, "Kangaroos can leap thirty feet in a single hop and travel more than thirty miles."

Ollie concluded, "I don't think I can keep up with kangaroos, but I can waddle with you anytime."

Mollie asked, "Is that animal over there another kangaroo?"

Ollie answered, "No, he is different. He is a wallaby."

Mollie replied, "He looks smaller and has a few more colors of fur."

Ollie stated, "Like kangaroos, wallabies are herbivores. They eat grasses and leaves."

Mollie mentioned, "I heard that a wallaby can be an Australian's pet. He can be very cuddly and will follow his owner around the house."

Mollie stated, "I love meeting animals who can be pets."

"Roar!" cried the lion.

"What was that sound?" questioned Ollie.

"It was the lion's roar," answered Mollie. "It can be heard five miles away."

"What do the lion and his cub eat?" asked Ollie.

"They are carnivores, so they eat only meat," stated Mollie.

"Is that the mommy or the daddy protecting the cub?" questioned Ollie.

"It is the cub's daddy because his mommy is out looking for food," answered Mollie.

"We better waddle away quietly so we won't be caught for their dinner," whispered Ollie.

"Ollie, I'm excited! I see an adorable cheetah and its cub," declared Mollie.

"Cheetahs run like the wind, faster than any animal I know," answered Ollie.

"Purr, purr!" cried the cheetahs.

"Did you hear them purring?" asked Mollie.

"They remind me of my cat back home," stated Ollie.

"I feel safe around the cheetah," whispered Mollie.

"Look at that soaring eagle!" shouted Mollie.

"The graceful bird is our national symbol of the United States," replied Ollie. "He is a symbol of freedom and peace."

"He is so elegant," stated Mollie. "I wonder why the bird is called a bald eagle."

"It is because his white head looks bald," answered Ollie. "The name comes from an English word *balde*, meaning 'white.'"

"How high can an eagle fly?" asked Mollie.

"Eagles fly with ease when they fly high in the air," answered Ollie. "They can glide as high as ten thousand feet."

"I admire the beauty of the eagles, and I am delighted that we encountered this enchanting bird," proclaimed Mollie.

"It feels so wonderful to be swimming," declared Mollie. "Be careful not to go too near the jellyfish. You might get stung," warned Ollie.

"Can the jellyfish see us?" asked Mollie.

"No, jellyfish do not have a brain, bones, eyes, or a heart," answered Ollie.

"I wonder how long jellyfish have been around," questioned Mollie.

"I heard jellyfish were here way before the dinosaurs," replied Ollie.

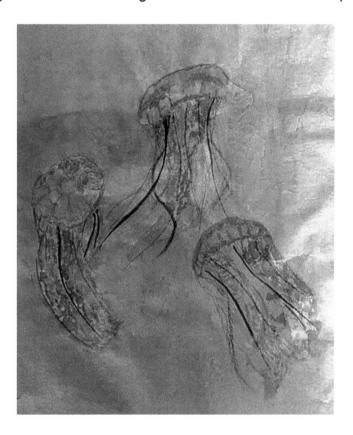

"Ollie, I'm scared of that gigantic hammerhead shark!" cried Mollie.

"We won't swim in his direction," answered Ollie.

"He looks like he has hundreds of teeth," exclaimed Mollie.

"Many sharks can have as many as three thousand teeth with five rows of teeth," explained Ollie. "They lose one hundred teeth each day."

"Wow, that is amazing! Does the shark have as many bones as teeth?" asked Mollie.

"Sharks don't have bones but cartilage, which is soft and muscular," answered Ollie.

"I can't believe sharks have been around for 440 million years," revealed Mollie.

"Sharks are so interesting, but I think we better go meet animals more like us," declared Ollie.

"I see those rabbits hopping over there," stated Mollie.

"Guess what? Rabbits can hop as high as three feet," replied Ollie.

"Unbelievable! By the way, how long are their ears?" asked Mollie.

"Would you believe four inches in length?" answered Ollie. "Rabbits can turn their ears halfway around watching out for predators."

"Purr, purr," murmured the rabbits.

"I love how the cuddly rabbits purr when they are cheerful," declared Mollie.

Ollie cried, "I love meeting all these darling dogs!"

Mollie declared, "If the dog licks you, that means he loves you."

Ollie replied, "A dog is smart. He can understand 250 words."

Mollie commented, "They understand our emotions like when we are joyful or sad."

Ollie shouted, "Let's stay around them forever!"

Mollie concluded, "They are man's best friend."

"I want to be friends with these sweet cats," declared Ollie.

"Cats are very intelligent," answered Mollie. "They can sleep with us because they sleep for thirteen to fourteen hours a day," replied Ollie.

"Meow," murmured the cat.

"Ollie, I think he wants our attention," whispered Mollie.

"They hear us chatting because cats have outstanding hearing and a wonderful sense of smell," stated Ollie.

"Let's stay awhile with these cats. They give me joy," voiced Mollie.

"We have met many lasting friends," revealed Ollie.

"Ollie, I see some birds that look like us, but they are smaller," declared Mollie. "They are the size of a soda can."

"They are called puffins. Unlike us, they can fly as fast as fifty-five miles per hour," stated Ollie.

"Both puffins and penguins are experienced swimmers," explained Mollie. "Puffins can dive thirty to forty feet, looking for fish."

"They can fetch up to sixty fish at one time," admired Ollie.

"Let's stay and become friends with these friendly puffins," proclaimed Mollie.

"What a magnificent world it is to have met so many unique animals and to have learned so much knowledge about them," revealed Mollie.

"I know, but it feels so wonderful to be back with penguins like us," declared Ollie.

"Let's go swimming and look for fish and krill," stated Mollie.

"Listen, I hear the penguins squawking. I dearly love those sounds," expressed Ollie.

"You and I can waddle over there and keep warm with our best friends," mentioned Mollie.

"There are seventeen different species of penguins in the world. But I love that we, the gentoo penguins, live in beautiful Antarctica," announced Ollie.

About the Author

Betty Oliver is a retired elementary school teacher of forty years. She earned her Bachelor of Science in Elementary Education and Master of Science in Education from Old Dominion University in Norfolk, Virginia. Betty Oliver lives in Virginia Beach, Virginia, with her miniature schnauzer. Betty loves to volunteer at the Children's Hospital of the King's Daughters in Norfolk, Virginia, and the surrounding hospitals with Ollie, her therapy dog. She also volunteers at the Virginia Aquarium in Virginia Beach. Her hobbies are tennis, art, and traveling the world. Her first book is *Travel the Seven Continents of the World with Ollie and Mollie*. Betty wanted to continue her adventures with Ollie and Mollie, so after her incredible trip to Egypt, she wrote her second book, *Travel to Egypt with Ollie and Mollie.*

She is the author and illustrator of her recent book, *Ollie and Mollie Meet New Friends*. Betty became an artist through her Japanese sumi-e classes. As one can tell from her new book, she loves painting all animals.

CPSIA information can be obtained
at www.ICGtesting.com
Printed in the USA
BVHW052122170222
629288BV00001B/13

9 781638 603153